SHRII BHAGAVAD GITA AND UPANISHAD CONNECTION

DR. JAGADEESH PILLAI

Copyright © Dr. Jagadeesh Pillai
All Rights Reserved.

This book has been self-published with all reasonable efforts taken to make the material error-free by the author. No part of this book shall be used, reproduced in any manner whatsoever without written permission from the author, except in the case of brief quotations embodied in critical articles and reviews.

The Author of this book is solely responsible and liable for its content including but not limited to the views, representations, descriptions, statements, information, opinions and references ["Content"]. The Content of this book shall not constitute or be construed or deemed to reflect the opinion or expression of the Publisher or Editor. Neither the Publisher nor Editor endorse or approve the Content of this book or guarantee the reliability, accuracy or completeness of the Content published herein and do not make any representations or warranties of any kind, express or implied, including but not limited to the implied warranties of merchantability, fitness for a particular purpose. The Publisher and Editor shall not be liable whatsoever for any errors, omissions, whether such errors or omissions result from negligence, accident, or any other cause or claims for loss or damages of any kind, including without limitation, indirect or consequential loss or damage arising out of use, inability to use, or about the reliability, accuracy or sufficiency of the information contained in this book.

Made with ♥ on the Notion Press Platform
www.notionpress.com

A tribute to all learners everywhere !!

Contents

Prayer   *vii*

About The Author   *ix*

Preface   *xv*

1. An Introduction To Bhagavad Gita And Upanishad   1
2. Renouncing The Battle   4
3. Integral Part Of Self-realization   6
4. Action And The Results   8
5. Attaining The Ultimate Knowledge   11
6. Surrendering To A Greater Purpose   14
7. Ideal Yogic Practice   16
8. Ultimate Truth About Self   18
9. Direct Knowledge Of The Self   21
10. Eternity Of Bliss Or Nirvana   23
11. Liberated To Access Pure Consciousness   25
12. Expansion Of Self-conciousness   28
13. God Devotion To Devotee   31
14. Understanding The Concept Of Brahman   33
15. Spiritual Practice And The Path Towards Attainment   36
16. Concept Of Ishvara And Its Sustenance   39
17. The Self And Core Of Consciousness   42
18. Ishwara (god) And The Jiva (individual Soul)   45
19. The Path Of Knowledge   47

Contents

20. Summary	49
Other Books Of The Author	51
Contact	53

Prayer

Om Poornamadah Poornamidam Poornat Poornamudachyate|
Poornasya Poornamadaya Poornamevavashisyate||
Om Shanti Shanti Shanti:||

About The Author

Dr. Jagadeesh Pillai four times Guinness World Record holder, a voracious reader, writer, and true research scholar was born in Varanasi, the abode of Lord Shiva. He is Ph.D. in Vedic Science. He is a multi-faceted polymath with innate qualities, creative ideas and many remarkable achievements. Although his roots extend back to "Gods own Country"(Kerala), the residents of Varanasi feel proud of him and adore him as a child of Varanasi who caters to every individual in need without any expectations. A deep study into his profile reflects that he has added so many feathers to his cap which makes him quite unique. He is a four times Guinness Book of World Records Holder in the following subjects :

1. "Script to Screen" which he achieved by producing and directing a state of art animation film within the shortest time possible by breaking the earlier set record by Canadians. There are many national and international Awards and Recognitions to his credit.

2. Longest Line of Post Cards which he has done on the occasion of 163 years of Indian Postal Day by 16300 post cards. The event was also connected with a questionnaire about Indian Flag.

3. Largest Poster Awareness Campaign – This was achieved by designing an awareness campaign on the subject "Beti Bachao – Beti Padhao".

4. Largest Envelop – Towards tribute to Prime Minister's initiative 'Make in India' – he has created about 4000 sq meter envelop using waste papers.

5. Attempted by lighting 70000 candles on a 210 kg cake to celebrate the 70th Indian Independence day recorded in World Records India.

6. Attempted a documentary on Dhamek Stupa of Sarnath dubbing in 17 languages, result is waiting from Guinness World Records.

He is versatile in Gita teaching. The young generation is fond of his Gita teaching and he has changed the life of many young through his continued motivational boost up and teachings.

He has composed and sung Gayatri Mantra in 1008 different tunes.

He has composed and sung Hanuman Chalisa in 108 different tunes.

He has composed and sung hundreds of Sanskrit Bhajans, Patriotic songs, etc.

He has written and directed so many short films and

documentaries for awareness campaigns.

He has done voluntary services to UP Police and Kerala Police to spread awareness campaigns on the various issue through videos and photography.

He is on the path of authoring thousands of books on Indian culture, Indian Temples, and the life of extraordinary people.

It is hard to believe that he has produced and directed more than 100 Documentaries on a particular city (Varanasi) which is done by a single person.

He has helped and guided more than 25 boys and girls to achieve world records through various creative and innovative methods.

A multifaceted person who can apply the best of his intellect using the God-given blessings which have been showered upon every human being granting them an immense capacity to learn, experience, and experiment with many things and do wonders in this world of discrimination and disparities.

He is a teacher and a student at the same time who always learns every day and teaches every day. As a master, his weakness was that he never sticks to a particular subject. Perhaps this weakness gives him the strength to master any area which he came across.

Each of his days dawned with learning a new topic and he spend most of his time experimenting and researching it.

ABOUT THE AUTHOR

He is also a selfless social activist and a motivational speaker.

His life was full of struggle, ups and downs, and failures. But he never gave up and faced all his trials and tribulations full of confidence. Today he is a successful young man with a lot of enthusiasm and rich life experience.

He has sung full Ram Charita Manas 51 hours audio by his own composition. He has also sung the whole Bhagavad-Gita in his own composition with a rhythmic background.

He has also sung "Lokah Samastha Sukhino Bhavantu" in 50 different languages.

Currently working on a detailed and scientific study on Veda, Upanishad, Puranas, Bhagavad Gita, etc.

He has composed and sung Hanuman Chalisa in 108 different compositions and Gayatri Mantra in 1008 different compositions.

Awards

Four Times Guinness World Records

Winner of Mahatma Gandhi Vishwa Shanti Puraskar

Mahatma Gandhi Global Peace Ambassador

Kashi Ratna Award

ABOUT THE AUTHOR

Dr. APJ Abdul Kalam Motivational Person of the Year 2017

Mother Teresa Award

Indira Gandhi Priyadarshini Award

Bharat Vikas Ratna Award

Udyog Ratna Award

Vigyan Prasar Award

Poorvanchal Ratn Samman

Preface

The Bhagavad Gita and Upanishads are two of the most important works in Hinduism, and they are deeply intertwined with each other. The Bhagavad Gita is a part of the Mahabharata epic, in which the warrior Arjuna is faced with a difficult moral dilemma. After much deliberation, Krishna, as his friend and advisor, gives Arjuna insight and advice based on the teachings found in Upanishadic texts. Thus, many of the concepts found in the Bhagavad Gita - such as reincarnation, dharma (duty), karma (action) and moksha (freedom from rebirth) - directly stem from ideas found in the Upanishadic tradition. Together, these two texts lay out the pattern for living a righteous life within Hinduism.

Without reading the Upanishads, we cannot gain a comprehensive understanding of the teachings of the Bhagavad Gita, as they are closely intertwined. In this book, I have made a humble attempt to explain each chapter of the Bhagavad Gita in relation to the Upanishads.

CHAPTER ONE

AN INTRODUCTION TO BHAGAVAD GITA AND UPANISHAD

The Bhagavad Gita and the Upanishads are two of the most important texts of Hindu philosophy. While the Bhagavad Gita is traditionally seen as a part of the Mahabharata, the Upanishads form part of the Vedas and are thus more ancient. Despite their breadth of time, these two sacred texts share common themes and ideas which bring them into conversation with one another. The Bhagavad Gita and the Upanishads convey a timeless wisdom on matters including karma, asceticism, meditation, and compassion for all living things. While the texts differ in their approach to these topics, there is a strong connection between them, emphasizing the importance of understanding and embracing their combined teachings.

One of the main topics explored by both the Bhagavad Gita and the Upanishads is karma. The Bhagavad Gita begins with a warrior, Arjuna, facing a difficult moral dilemma as he prepares to go to battle. Lord Krishna gives him guidance, teaching him that by dedicating his action to Him and acting out of dharma (righteousness), his karma will remain untainted. In the Upanishads, this idea is further developed through the concept of Brahman, in which all actions are performed as a part of an overarching divine plan, and all karma is karmically connected in a vast cosmic web. Ultimately, both texts emphasize the importance of understanding karma and acting with dharma in everyday life, leading to a more harmonious existence.

Asceticism is another important topic explored in both the Bhagavad Gita and the Upanishads. In the Gita, Krishna encourages Arjuna to practice spiritual austerity (tapas) as a way to become "fixed in divine intelligence." On the other hand, the Upanishads portray asceticism as a means of escaping the cycle of suffering and achieving Moksha, or liberation, by renouncing the physical world and turning one's focus to the divine. Thus, while the Upanishads present asceticism as a path to enlightenment, the Bhagavad Gita invites us to incorporate its principles into our daily lives as a way to cultivate spiritual wellness.

The Bhagavad Gita and the Upanishads both emphasize the importance of meditation as a tool for spiritual realization. The Gita outlines various paths including mantra japa (chanting Vedic hymns), meditation on the divine, and the practice of self-inquiry (atma-vichara). Similarly, the Upanishads prescribe meditative techniques to reach enlightenment including breath control, focusing on the individual soul, and inner reflection. While the Gita provides more accessible techniques, the Upanishads offer a deeper insight into the process of meditation as a way to understand and transcend the material world.

DR. JAGADEESH PILLAI

CHAPTER TWO

Renouncing the Battle

The Bhagavad Gita's first chapter is deeply connected to many of the Upanishads, especially the Isha Upanishad. This is because the larger context of the Bhagavad Gita is drawn from the Upanishads, which themselves contain Vedic knowledge and wisdom. One of the key features of the first chapter of the Bhagavad Gita is its poetic language, which is used effectively to draw on the ideas of the Upanishads and other sources.

The chapter begins with Arjuna asking Krishna a difficult question about renouncing the battle and the impending death of both his own family and his enemies. This question is found directly in the Isha Upanishad in the passage "What should one do to attain complete realization?" It is apparent from the context of Arjuna's question that he is searching for enlightened knowledge, which can be found in the Upanishads especially in kathopanishad.

Drawing further on the Upanishads, Krishna uses the chapter to discuss the concept of liberation or moksha. He explains that the body is not the Self of one's being, rather the Atman or essence of the soul is the true Self.

This is similar to the Upanishad concept of the Atman, which is the higher self that exists beyond the physical body. By rejecting the body and the material world, Krishna encourages Arjuna to recognize and accept his true Self and gain liberation from negative attachments.

In the chapter, Krishna also discusses Dharma or the unique path of duty for each individual. It is found in the Upanishads that everyone has their own unique Dharma, according to their social and material wealth, knowledge, and moral conduct. By adhering to one's Dharma and fulfilling their specific obligations, it is possible to reach realization and gain moksha. In this way, the Bhagavad Gita connects to the Upanishads.

The chapter then moves on to discuss the concepts of action (Karma), mindfulness (samadhi), and devotion to the divine (bhakti). Each of these principles is found in the various Upanishads, and the first chapter of the Bhagavad Gita serves to bring all of these concepts together in a single place.

Overall, it is clear that the first chapter of the Bhagavad Gita is deeply connected to the various Upanishads. By drawing on the ideas of the Upanishads, Krishna is able to give insight and wisdom to Arjuna. Ultimately, by understanding and recognizing the true Self in all things, it is possible for Arjuna to gain genuine liberation.

CHAPTER THREE

Integral Part of Self-realization

The Bhagavad Gita, a sacred Hindu text, is well known for its collection of philosophical verses, which greatly serve to highlight the essence of spirituality and dharma. Its second chapter specifically deals with the concept of Upanishad, which is a term used to refer to the "secret doctrine" within Hinduism.

Within this chapter, there is an illuminating conversation between Arjuna, a great warrior, and Lord Krishna, who is known as an incarnation of the Divine. Here, Arjuna expresses confusion and bewilderment regarding his current state, to which Krishna answers by asking him to stop depending on external circumstances and open his eyes to the inherent knowledge inside of himself. This Upanishadic Knowledge provides Arjuna with the realization that he is not just a warrior, but rather a spiritual being that can transcend the boundaries of time and space.

The second chapter of the Bhagavad Gita is essentially a dialogue between Krishna and Arjuna, which serves to unravel the inner workings of Arjuna's being. Through this, the reader is introduced to the Upanishadic Knowledge, which is presented as an integral part of self-realization. According to the teachings of the text, this knowledge reminds individuals of the true, eternal nature of the self. This is in stark contrast to our temporal understanding of the world, providing us with the means to rise above material existence and go beyond the limits of human understanding.

The Upanishadic Knowledge taught in the second chapter of the Bhagavad Gita is best compared with Buddhism, particularly the four noble truths which are meant to elucidate a sense of truth and freedom. In the same way, the Upanishadic Knowledge aids Arjuna in understanding his true spiritual nature, resulting in liberation and peace. In addition, the chapter also touches on various other aspects of the Upanishads such as the concepts of Atman, Brahman, and the underlying purpose of life. Thus, it serves to reveal the essence of Upanishadic thought, which is ultimately concerned with the attainment of self-realization.

To conclude, the second chapter of the Bhagavad Gita serves to introduce its readers to the Upanishadic Knowledge and the concept of inner enlightenment. Through the dialogue between Lord Krishna and Arjuna, the reader is exposed to the essence of self-realization and the concepts which are integral to a fuller understanding of the self. In this way, it can thereby be seen that this chapter has an immense connection with Upanishad.

CHAPTER FOUR

Action and The Results

The Bhagavad Gita is a treasured ancient Indian text said to be one of the main sources of spiritual wisdom. Its timeless lessons have been discussed and appreciated by generations of people around the world, and its contents have an important connection to the Upanishads. The third chapter of the Bhagavad Gita is particularly significant due to its close ties to the Upanishads and its exploration of the relationship of the soul to God.

The concept of yoga is discussed in the third chapter of the Bhagavad Gita, and it is closely connected to the Upanishads. The Upanishads are an essential source of knowledge that represents the ancient Vedic philosophical teachings and is believed to contain the essence of the ancient Hindu spiritual path. Yoga, as explained in the third chapter of the Bhagavad Gita, is the binding of the individual spirit to the divine spirit, thereby joining them together in perfect harmony. The Upanishads provide further insight into the relationship between individual souls, or Atman, and the Supreme Soul, the Parmatman. This connection is highlighted in the third chapter of the Bhagavad Gita, as the relationship between the soul and God is explored.

The third chapter of the Bhagavad Gita focuses on the nature of Brahman, the universal being. Brahman is identified as both the material and spiritual aspects of the world, and the Upanishads illuminate further on the qualities of Brahman. The third chapter of the Bhagavad Gita reveals that Brahman is endowed with all qualities, and the Upanishads further explain that Brahman is the source of all creation. This idea is further discussed in the Bhagavad Gita, where it is stated that Brahman is the source of all knowledge, power and action.

The third chapter of the Bhagavad Gita goes on to discuss the nature of worshipping God and the results that can come of it. The Upanishads offer further insight into this idea, explaining that those who worship God will be blessed with the joy that comes from living in the spiritual realm. This joy is said to be unfathomable and beyond the comprehension of ordinary humans. The third chapter of the Bhagavad Gita further explores the idea of yoga as a means of uniting the individual and God. It explains that with true devotion and focus, the individual can achieve a state of perfect harmony and oneness with Brahman.

The third chapter of the Bhagavad Gita has a close connection to the Upanishads and the ancient Hindu spiritual path. The third chapter explains the concept of yoga in great detail and the Upanishads deepen the exploration by discussing the relationship of individual souls and the Supreme Soul. These two sacred texts work together to harmoniously explore the nature of Brahman and the spiritual journey that each individual soul can take to be united with God.

CHAPTER FIVE

Attaining the Ultimate Knowledge

The fourth chapter of the Bhagavad Gita is an important part of the sacred Hindu scripture, and offers a deep spiritual connection to the Upanishads. The chapter is titled "Jnana-yog", meaning the Yoga of Knowledge and is aimed at helping mankind in understanding the world and the connection between the self and the world. The Upanishads offer a similar insight into this connection and are characterized by their quest to seek knowledge in order to arrive at the truth about life and its purpose. Both the Bhagavad Gita and the Upanishads offer a similar path to knowledge, which is through inner reflection and contemplation.

In the fourth chapter of the Bhagavad Gita, Arjuna and Krishna form a dialogue in which Krishna attempts to assist Arjuna in attaining the ultimate knowledge. Krishna speaks of the essence of life, which he describes as being atman—the soul or the eternal self. He reveals that atman is the source of knowledge and happiness, and thus true contentment lies within our own being. In a similar vein, the Upanishads encourage us to try to access this inner knowledge, suggesting that there is something hidden within us and our task is to discover it.

A central theme in the Bhagavad Gita fourth chapter is that of self-control. Krishna encourages Arjuna to attempt to restrain his senses so he can attain wisdom and knowledge. He further explains that when senses are kept under control we are no longer attached to our physical desires and passions, and thus we can lead a life free from suffering and unhappiness. This is eerily similar to the concepts outlined in the Upanishads, which attempt to free us from bondage and alienation from our true self.

The fourth chapter of the Bhagavad Gita also speaks of Arjuna's duty, or dharma. Dharma is defined in this chapter as the natural laws which we must abide by in order to attain the ultimate knowledge. Essentially, we need to pursue the right kind of knowledge and practice the right kind of behavior in order to tap into our inner knowledge. This is similar to the idea of the moral law in the Upanishads and speaks to the idea of being in tune with the natural order of the world.

Thus, we can see that there is a deeply spiritual and philosophical connection between the fourth chapter of the Bhagavad Gita and the Upanishads. Both share a common goal of helping mankind gain knowledge and understanding, with this knowledge ultimately leading to a state of true contentment. By embracing the courage to explore our inner selves and understanding the moral responsibility we have when striving for the truth, we can begin to gain a deeper understanding of life, its purpose and our innermost self.

DR. JAGADEESH PILLAI

CHAPTER SIX

Surrendering to a Greater Purpose

The fifth chapter of the Bhagavad Gita is closely connected with the Upanishads, which are ancient Hindu works containing core Hindu philosophical beliefs. The Upanishads are collections of sacred passages and teachings that provide a foundation for many areas of Hindu practice, including spiritual knowledge and wisdom. In the Bhagavad Gita, the fifth chapter, known as Uddhava Gita, is closely related to the Upanishads, providing an especially vivid interpretation of the teachings contained therein.

The Uddhava Gita is filled with numerous references to Upanishadic concepts, its language and ideas echoing the most important teachings of the Upanishads. This includes references to the Brahman, Atman, the path of Self-realisation, the concentration of unalloyed devotion and the importance of liberation.

The main themes of the Uddhava Gita's teachings demonstrate a clear connection to the general themes found in the Upanishads. The primary theme is that of seeking knowledge, of deepening understanding and ultimately being liberated from suffering. The importance of knowledge is paramount in the teachings of both the Upanishads and the Uddhava Gita. Knowledge is seen as a means of unlocking the way to liberation and of transcending the limitations of earthly life. The Uddhava Gita also touches on the importance of self-control, of disciplining the body and the mind, in order to clear the path to Self-realisation. This too is an Upanishadic theme, emphasizing the need to overcome attachments to material objects and desires.

Moreover, the Uddhava Gita demonstrates the necessity of surrendering to a greater purpose when striving towards Self-realisation, a teaching derived directly from the Upanishads. By surrendering to something higher, such as the Supreme Being, we are able to unlock our true potential, to live out our highest purpose and to rise above limiting beliefs and expectations.

The fifth chapter of the Bhagavad Gita has an unmistakable connection to the Upanishads and to the teachings of Hinduism in general. Through its vivid imagery and specific references to the core teachings of the Upanishads, the Uddhava Gita serves as an important reminder of the need to strive towards a greater purpose and to continuously seek knowledge and understanding. Ultimately, both the Upanishads and the Uddhava Gita seek to provide us with guidance and a higher understanding of life, teaching us to live with purpose and to reach beyond our limits.

CHAPTER SEVEN

Ideal Yogic Practice

The Bhagavad Gita, also known as the Song of God, is a timeless Hindu scripture from the Mahabharata. The sixth chapter of the Gita, known as the Sanjaya-Gita, contains many significant connections with the Upanishads, the traditional philosophical texts of Hinduism. In this chapter, Lord Krishna instructs Arjuna, the main protagonist of the Mahabharata epic, in the paths of wisdom and self-realization.

The opening verses of the sixth chapter of the Gita emphasize the importance of yoga, particularly in its spiritual aspects. In these verses, in line with the Upanishads, Lord Krishna articulates the Supreme Truth as an absolute oneness, equating the individual's existence, commitment and dedication to the Absolute oneness. This alludes to the Advaita concept, a central tenet of the Upanishads, which emphasizes the unity between Self and Brahman (the divine). Moreover, ideal yogic practice affirmed in the Gita encourages the individual to go beyond the level of their material identity and move towards a higher state of consciousness, which is in line with principal Upanishadic teachings.

The discussions of the Gita in relation to karma are also extensively linked to the teachings of the Upanishads. The Upanishads emphasize that karma is the law of cause and effect, and is an irrevocable force that governs all of our actions, whether good or bad. In the sixth chapter of the Gita, Lord Krishna builds upon this fundamental belief and encourages Arjuna to use it to his advantage in order to free himself of materialistic desires and motivations, and become liberated from worldly ties. He reminds him that while it is impossible to escape the consequences of one's actions, it is in his best interests to focus on the spiritual aspects of life, rather than the material.

Finally, the sixth chapter of the Gita also contains a discussion of the importance of equanimity and non-attachment, both of which are essential Upanishadic teachings. The Gita encourages Arjuna to practice detachment from desires and worldly matters in order for him to achieve the state of inner peace and sameness, living in harmony and in tune with the Divine. This is in line with Upanishadic beliefs of letting go of all attachments, desires and limiting beliefs, to discover the blissful inner peace of the soul.

In conclusion, the sixth chapter of the Bhagavad Gita is deeply connected to the philosophical teachings of the Upanishads. Through its teachings on yoga, karma and detachment, the Gita provides us with a wealth of insight into the eternal truths of the Upanishads, offering us a glimpse into the spiritual truth of existence.

CHAPTER EIGHT

Ultimate Truth about Self

The Bhagavat Gita is one of the most important and foundational religious texts in Hinduism and one of the most widely read and revered philosophical works in all of Indian literature. The Gita has found resonance with a wide diversity of religious and philosophical views, and has been sought out by seekers of spiritual enlightenment and religious devotion across India, Asia and the world at large. The seventh chapter of the Bhagavat Gita is focused primarily on the concept of the Self, which is a fundamental teaching of the Upanishads.

The Gita's seventh chapter opens with Arjuna, the story's protagonist, asking Krishna, the story's divine teacher, about the true nature of the Self. In response, Krishna reveals the Ultimate Truth about Self, which is at the heart of the Upanishad teachings. The Self is one, unique, and eternal, and it transcends all material objects and worldly attachments. It is the driving force behind all of existence and inherent in all living things. As Krishna states in the Gita, the Self is both "the lord of all beings and the giver of all things." In essence, it is the core of the Ultimate reality of existence.

Krishna further explains that because all of existence is really a single unified Self, it is not subject to the laws of cause and effect. Indeed, the Upanishads present the notion of non-duality, which states that everything in existence is really One, and is therefore beyond the laws of causality. Thus, happiness and suffering are merely projections of the mind and do not really exist outside of our thoughts. The Upanishads also assert that all knowledge, material and spiritual, originate from the Self and that by discovering the true Self, one is able to transcend the material world and realize true freedom and eternal bliss.

Krishna then states the main teaching of the Bhagavat Gita: that the path to liberation from the cycles of suffering and reincarnation is to shift focus away from worldly attachments and instead devote one's being to the service of the Divine. The Upanishads also encourage this devotion to "God", as the Self is the source of Truth that is beyond all material and worldly concerns. One of the most salient themes of the Upanishad philosophy is to develop love and surrender to the Divine, in order to move closer to the unity of Self.

The seventh chapter of the Bhagavat Gita is a concise and comprehensive summary of the major teachings of the Upanishads. Its timeless message of selflessness and devotion to the divine is likely what continues to make it one of the most widely read and venerated philosophical texts throughout the world. Its connection with the Upanishads serves to provide an even deeper understanding of its teachings and to reinforce the strong similarities between the two ancient philosophical works.

CHAPTER NINE

Direct Knowledge of the Self

The eighth chapter of the Bhagavad Gita, also known as Kishkinda-kanda Parva, is closely linked to the teachings of the Upanishads. The Upanishads are ancient Hindu scriptures which contain spiritual teachings meant to help one become liberated and attain Self-Realization or moksha. The eighth chapter of the Gita not only expounds on the teachings of the Upanishads but also provides an incredible synthesis of its own that unites the different schools of Vedanta philosophy.

The essence of the Upanishads is the oneness of Brahman and Atman, the Unmanifest from which everything originates. In the eight chapter of Gita, Lord Krishna affirms this ultimate truth expressing his divine nature and encouraging Arjuna to seek the knowledge of Brahman. Lord Krishna is described as the teacher of the six ancient sages and the source of the knowledge of the Vedas. He then declares himself to be the source of all knowledge, granting Arjuna a deeper understanding of the Self, which is essential to the path of liberation.

Lord Krishna further explains how true freedom is achieved through direct knowledge of the Self and by surrendering to the divine force. He gives Arjuna an overview of the process of spiritual liberation, emphasizing the importance of understanding the supreme Reality and its distinction from the illusory world of the senses. He also explains the importance of realizing the oneness of the Divine and the Self without being attached to worldly accomplishments.

The eighth chapter of the Gita ultimately brings together the teachings of the Upanishads with the Vedanta schools. It is considered one of the most important texts as it provides us with a synthesis of different Hindu metaphysics and spiritual philosophies. It imbeds the Upanishadic understanding of Brahman into the path of liberation and does so in a way that brings together the different strands of Vedanta, unifying the various schools of thought.

The eighth chapter is an essential part of the Gita and an essential part of Indian spiritual philosophy. It deeply clarifies the knowledge found in the Upanishads, providing a path for achieving true freedom. Through its powerful teachings, it unites the paths of dharma, yoga, and jnana and opens up the path of liberation. It is a gift to all seekers of truth, as it clearly details the path for us to experience the oneness of Brahman.

CHAPTER TEN

Eternity of Bliss or Nirvana

The ninth chapter of the Bhagavad Gita is a very important section of the epic Hindu philosophical text. It introduces the concept of Yoga, and is heavily related to the Upanishads, a collection of ancient texts considered to be the fountainhead of the Vedic philosophical tradition. The Upanishads are a source of knowledge for the spiritual seeker and discuss the relationship between the human and divine. The Bhagavad Gita's ninth chapter stands as a bridge between these two great texts.

The chapter starts with Arjuna asking Krishna how to attain infinity, which can be taken to mean either an eternity of bliss or Nirvana. To answer his query, Krishna presents the teachings of Yoga, which he describes as the science of the soul. He explains eight parts of Yoga to Arjuna: Yama, Niyama, Asana, Pranayama, Pratyahara, Dhyana, Dharana, and Samadhi. These are the branches of Yoga practiced by the Upanishadic seers. Yoga is presented as an art of union between the microcosm of the individual and the macrocosm of the Universe. Using the four means of spiritual progress, namely Dharma (righteousness), Jnana (knowledge), Bhakti (love) and Karma (action), an individual can awaken the divine spirit within. Through the perfect control of body, breath, and mind, one is able to transcend the body, mind and ego and move towards an ultimate union with the divine.

What is remarkable is that not only does Krishna discuss the concepts of Yoga with Arjuna, he also provides related instructions from the Upanishads. For example, he tells Arjuna to seek the divine within, to practice spiritual exercises, to meditate, to control bodily functions and to renounce material desires. All of these instructions can be found in the Upanishads. Similarly, the description of the yogic ideal presented in this chapter, that of an unflinching, detached, contemplative seeker, coincides with the philosophy found in the Upanishads.

In conclusion, the ninth chapter of the Bhagavad Gita contains several important connections to the Upanishads. It serves as a bridge between these two texts, providing a comprehensive overview of the spiritual practice of Yoga. The teachings provided in this chapter can be used as a source of spiritual guidance, helping people to grow towards union with the divine.

CHAPTER ELEVEN

Liberated to Access Pure Consciousness

The Bhagavad-Gita's Tenth Chapter has been described as the climax of the dialogue between Krishna and Arjuna. This chapter is a powerful exposition of Vedanta, and is closely connected to the Upanishads. In this chapter, Krishna unveils truths that form the core of Upanishadic teaching and Vedanta philosophy, showing Arjuna that one can be liberated from the cycle of life and death by becoming a true yogi.

Krishna presents His Vishvarupa, the Universal Form, to Arjuna, revealing His true divine nature. He is both the Absolute Brahman and the Supreme Being, and can be perceived in different ways according to one's attitude and understanding. By seeing His true form, Arjuna is overwhelmed and Krishna teaches him the principles of perceiving Brahman, perspective and meditation through His Vishvarupa. This teaching is very similar to what is found in several Upanishads.

Krishna then outlines the core principle of non-dualism, showing Arjuna how the truly realized yogi is no longer bound by body, mind, or ego and, instead is liberated to access pure consciousness. This idea is fundamental to Upanishadic understanding, and is based on the theory that Brahman, or the Absolute, is the source of all that is, and all creation is a single, unified whole. Thus, in order to attain moksha, or enlightenment, one must recognize that all of creation, including oneself, is part of this unified whole. Furthermore, Krishna teaches Arjuna the importance of controlling desires, as they too bind the practitioner to the physical world and hinder spiritual growth.

Krishna also clearly conveys the importance of understanding the body mind connection and of following the right path to spiritual knowledge. He outlines the four paths of yoga: jnana yoga, bhakti yoga, raja yoga and karma yoga. These paths are directly linked to the Upanishadic teachings, as they all lead to finding union with Brahman. This is a teaching found in several Upanishads, and it is further solidified in the Bhagavad-Gita's Tenth Chapter.

Finally, Krishna offers Arjuna assurance that he does not need to fear death, as death is merely a transition from one life to the next and can be overcome by understanding that the soul is eternal, and beyond the material world. This is one of the most important teachings of Upanishadic philosophy, and one that is deeply explored in this chapter.

The Bhagavad-Gita's Tenth Chapter is thus an essential part of Vedantic and Upanishadic teachings. It outlines the fundamental principles of Upanishadic philosophy, including the concept of unity, understanding the body mind connection and the importance of right actions, as well as the eternal nature of the soul.

DR. JAGADEESH PILLAI

CHAPTER TWELVE

Expansion of Self-Conciousness

The Bhagavad Gita is a sacred Hindu philosophical text, written in Sanskrit and part of the Hindu epic Mahabharata. The 11th chapter of the Bhagavad Gita is often referred to as the "Vision of the Universal Form" and is about Krishna's revelation of his divine form and his teachings of karma yoga to Arjuna. It is a chapter that is closely connected to the Upanishads, a collection of sacred texts belonging to the Vedanta tradition and an important part of Hindu scripture. The relationship between these two is that the Bhagavad Gita is understood to be the practical application of the Upanishadic philosophy to the particular situation of the warrior class in ancient India.

The Upanishads are the source of the Vedantic philosophy which is the foundation of Krishna's teachings in the Bhagavad Gita. One of the basic concepts which is expressed clearly in the Upanishads is the idea of Atman, the eternal and unchanging self, which is also expressed in the Bhagavad Gita when Krishna speaks of Arjuna's inner self. This concept is expressed in the 11th chapter when Krishna reveals his divine form and explains that although all creatures are part of himself he remains separate. This is expressed in the highest way in this chapter as the Upanishads would in the ancient period, but in a more practical way.

The Bhagavad Gita, as a part of the Hindu Upanishadic tradition, recommends practical behavior based on the principle of karma yoga. It is in the 11th chapter that Krishna talks of the importance of this practice for freeing one of their accumulated karma and achieving enlightenment. This is, again, closely connected with Upanishadic philosophy, particularly the notion of the importance of performing ones' obligations free from attachment and expectant of no reward. This idea is reiterated in the Bhagavad Gita and it is clear that the texts, as part of the same philosophical tradition, have very similar messages.

Finally, the 11th chapter of the Bhagavad Gita can be seen in connection with the Upanishads in terms of devotion to God. Here, Arjuna is exposed to a part and an extension of himself which represents the highest form of devotion; an understanding of the unity between all life and the divine power which guides it. This experience is comparable to that expressed in many Upanishads where seekers of moksha or liberation acquire a comprehensive and all-encompassing understanding of their Atman or self.

The Devi-bhagavata Purana describes the Bhagavad Gita as a divinely revealed scripture which is above all the Vedas and Upanishads and as such it is clear that the two are deeply connected.

CHAPTER THIRTEEN

God Devotion to Devotee

The Bhagavad Gita is one of India's most widely known and influential religious texts. It is a companion poem to the Indian epic, "The Mahabharata", into which it was incorporated between 200 BCE and 200 CE. It is a work that has had an immense influence on Hindu philosophy, religion, culture, and spirituality.

The twelfth chapter of the Bhagavad Gita is devoted to the concept of "Brahman", which is the highest reality. It is considered to be the supreme form of existence, existing outside of time, space, and causality. The chapter begins by discussing the nature of Brahman and its relationship to the human soul. It then moves on to extol the virtues of those who embrace the teachings of Brahman and live as spiritual seekers.

One of the primary ways in which the twelfth chapter of the Bhagavad Gita connects to the Upanishads is in its emphasis on the concept of "atman", or the individual soul. It is this individual soul that is seen to be connected to the greater reality of Brahman. The chapter states that the souls of the spiritual seekers find freedom and joy in realizing the oneness of their individual selves and Brahman. It teaches that Brahman is the source of all life, and that those who surrender to Brahman will find their ultimate liberation.

The chapter also contains many of the same principles that are found in the Upanishads. This includes the ideas of karma, Samsara, and moksha as instruments for attaining liberation. The chapter further proclaims that all living beings are one and that through the path of self-realization, one can overcome obstacles and attain emancipation.

Lastly, the twelfth chapter of the Bhagavad Gita also emphasizes the power of meditation and contemplation as the path to achieving realization. It speaks of the need to open one's eyes to the true nature of reality, and to understand the nature of Brahman. It explains that the ultimate purpose of life is to know and comprehend the truth, and that service to others is the highest form of spiritual practice.

In conclusion, it can be seen that the twelfth chapter of the Bhagavad Gita has strong connections to the Upanishads. Through its teachings on the concept of Brahman and its emphasis on self-realization, the chapter provides an important source of insight into the spiritual journey. Its practices of meditation and self-surrender serve to guide and provide comfort to those seeking to reach their ultimate freedom in Brahman.

CHAPTER FOURTEEN

Understanding the Concept of Brahman

The Bhagavad Gita is one of the most influential texts of Hinduism and is a distillation of the essence of the Upanishads. Chapter 13 of the Gita is essential for establishing the close connection between the Upanishads and the Gita. The two texts form a powerful synthesis of metaphysics, ethics, and spiritual practice, providing an insight into the complexity and depth of Hindu thought.

The core thesis of Chapter 13 of the Gita is the teaching of what is commonly referred to as the "synthetic Vedanta", which firmly connects the Upanishads with the Bhagavad Gita. The Gita explains the concept of Brahman, the Absolute Reality and Supreme Being. Brahman is described in the text as being beyond the grasp of the mind, and it is neither deistic nor pantheistic in structure. The goal of the Synthetic Vedanta is to unite the Upanishads with the Bhagavad Gita, by showing the oneness of reality, as expressed by Brahman.

The Indian sage Sri Aurobindo states that the Upanishads teach of a "mystical Vedanta of union with the One", while the Bhagavad Gita provides the direction of how to move from the manifested world to that union. Chapter 13 of the Bhagavad Gita combines both of these foundations, linking the unity of Brahman through Yoga and devotion. The Gita explains that the individual soul is connected to Brahman, the Absolute, and is responsible for cultivating its knowledge and understanding to reach the ultimate reality and be one with Brahman.

The term Yoga is used throughout Chapter 13 of the Gita and becomes an important part in understanding the concept of Brahman, and establishing the connection between the Upanishads and the Gita. Yoga is considered to be a discipline by which one can gain insight into the true nature of reality. The Gita explains that one can use the practice of Yoga to seek only the truth and to try to reach a higher level of consciousness, through the eight limbs of Yoga.

Finally, Chapter 13 of the Bhagavad Gita concludes by focusing on devotion and providing insight into the importance of devotional practice. Several verses of the Gita explain that the highest form of knowledge comes through devotional practice to God and His manifestations. Devotional practice is necessary in order to connect with the Absolute, and therefore fulfill the purpose of the Synthetic Vedanta, to unite the Upanishads with the Bhagavad Gita.

In conclusion, Chapter 13 of the Bhagavad Gita establishes the close connection between the Upanishads and the Gita. It explains the concept of Brahman, the Absolute Reality and Supreme Being, and provides an insight into the

Synthetic Vedanta, by synthesizing the philosophies laid out by the Upanishads and the Bhagavad Gita.

CHAPTER FIFTEEN

Spiritual Practice and the Path Towards Attainment

The Bhagavad Gita's fourteenth chapter is one of the most well-known texts of the Upanishads. This sacred text has become an integral part of Hindu spiritual practice due to its powerful and timeless teachings. The Bhagavad Gita's fourteenth chapter, titled Samkhya Yoga, is composed of seventy-five verses, each of which contain an important lesson or essence. It is composed in a conversational style between the Lord Krishna and the warrior-prince Arjuna, and each of its seventy-five verses offer a lesson regarding the highest teachings of Upanishad thought.

The main point of the fourteenth chapter of the Bhagavad Gita is to explain the ways of attaining knowledge and liberation. As a central part of the Upanishads, this chapter teaches about the importance of self-realization, understanding both one's true nature and the nature of the universe. This pursuit of self-knowledge is achievable through the practice of yoga and meditation. According to the Bhagavad Gita, 'yoga is the journey of the self, through the self, to the self'.

The fourteenth chapter further emphasizes that a person's liberation comes from the discovery of the true self. It explains that only by doing away with attachments and desires, both physical and mental, can one realize his true self. Also, it states that the realized person, liberated from the cycle of birth and death, will gain insight into the Nature of God, or the Supreme Self. It goes on to say that true knowledge is knowledge of one's own divine essence and union with the divine, which leads to eternal peace and joy.

The fourteenth chapter of the Bhagavad Gita also discusses the differences between knowledge (jnana) and work (karma). It explains that knowledge is superior to work and that true knowledge leads to liberation. It further explains that knowledge is gained through Vedic scriptures, the teachings of sages, meditation, and other spiritual practice. Knowledge is gained from within, through the pure consciousness present within each soul, without attachment or expectation of reward.

The Bhagavad Gita's fourteenth chapter is intricately connected to the Upanishads in its teachings about knowledge, detachment, and liberation. By emphasising the practice of yoga, meditation and self-realization, this chapter provides powerful insight into spiritual practice and the path towards attainment of liberation. It is an essential part of Hindu thought and has stood the test of time as one of the most important sacred texts of the Upanishads.

CHAPTER SIXTEEN

Concept of Ishvara and its Sustenance

The Bhagavad Gita, an essential part of Hinduism, is an ancient Sanskrit text that comprises eighteen chapters of the epic Mahabharata. In the Gita, Lord Krishna expounds on the spiritual wisdom to his friend and devotee, Arjuna. The fifteenth chapter, Vaishnavadhikaranasamasa, is often linked to the Upanishads due to its emphasis on the importance of divine realization.

The Bhagavad Gita is known for its emphasis on the divine realization of Self. The fifteenth chapter of the Gita further emphasizes this notion as Lord Krishna imparts a knowledge of creation to his devotee Arjuna. He explains that the physical world is only a mere representation of the higher divine plane of consciousness. He acknowledges that without reaching inner truth and divine realization, one will meet with the hand of God's wrath. The fifteenth chapter of the Gita explains that God, whose form is never seen, is nonetheless all-pervasive. He creates and destroys this material world continuously but is unaffected by it. This is similar to the teachings in the Upanishads which explain the divine nature of reality.

The fifteenth chapter of the Bhagavad Gita also talks about the concept of Ishvara (God). Lord Krishna reveals to Arjuna that the material world is created through Ishvara and relies on him for its sustenance. Furthermore, Arjuna is schooled on the five forms of Ishvara and their powers. The Upanishads also refer to the concept of Ishvara as the source of all that exists. This includes both the material and non-material realms, from the animate and inanimate entities to the stars, planets, and galaxies. This is further elucidated in the fifteenth chapter of the Bhagavad Gita as Lord Krishna describes the multiple forms of Ishvara and their capabilities.

The fifteenth chapter of the Bhagavad Gita also outlines the components of devotional service. The concept of Bhakti yoga is discussed in this chapter and Lord Krishna elaborates on the importance of knowledge and devotion in attaining divine realization. This is a concept that is also found in the Upanishads, as they contain numerous scriptures on the virtues of dedication and selfless service to God.

In summary, the fifteenth chapter of the Bhagavad Gita has strong connections with the Upanishads. Both texts emphasize the importance of understanding the divine nature of reality and the power of devotional service to reach a state of divine realization. The concept of Ishvara and its multiple forms are discussed in both the Gita and Upanishads, as are the outcomes of attaining realization. In this way, the fifteenth chapter of the Gita can be seen as a continuation of the spiritual wisdom imparted in the Upanishads.

CHAPTER SEVENTEEN

The self and Core of consciousness

The Bhagavad Gita 16th Chapter is often seen as a bridge between the Upanishads and the rest of the Gita. It deals with the nature of the Atman (Soul) and, in particular, its relationship to the body and the physical world, setting the stage for the rest of the Gita.

The 16th chapter begins with Arjuna asking Lord Krishna whether the Atman, the indwelling self, is destroyed at the time of death, or whether it passes on to some other world. Krishna answers that the soul never dies, but that it is indestructible, everlasting, and imperishable. He explains that although the body is destroyed and the individual soul enters a new body, the Atman — the self and core of consciousness — remains the same. This answer echoes one of the key concepts of the Upanishads – that of the immortal and eternally unchanging soul that neither dies nor is recomposed during physical death.

Krishna emphasizes his point by using examples from the Upanishads and the Vedic scriptures — often in conjunction with scriptural metaphors and images. For example, he mentions the rebirth of the individual soul — a long-standing theme in the Upanishads. He also speaks of the Atman assuming different forms, which is reminiscent of the idea of the Atman being like a spark of fire in the Upanishadic texts. These examples suggest a close relationship between the Bhagvad Gita 16th Chapter and the Upanishads.

Moreover, the chapter informs us of the moral values and spiritual practices taught in the Upanishads, such as meditation, austerity, and the cultivation of wisdom. The teachings in this chapter remind one of the many conversations involving Krishna and Arjuna in the Upanishads. These exchanges teach us that it is through choosing our way in life and applying various spiritual disciplines that we can obtain the knowledge and insight of the ultimate reality.

The 16th chapter reveals to us that our soul remains inherently pure and untouched by the changes in our body and mind. This truth has been portrayed in the fourteenth verse of the Bhagavad Gita, which proclaims that the Atman can never be destroyed. This confirms what is stated in the Upanishads — that despite whatever changes occur in our life, the Atman remains the same.

Clearly, the Bhagvad Gita 16th Chapter has a direct connection with the Upanishads. In it, the concept of the immortal soul and its relation to death, rebirth, and the physical world are thoroughly discussed. Moreover, it speaks of moral and spiritual practices taught in the Upanishads and shows us that it is through these practices that one can gain insight into the supreme truth. It reveals to us that, although the body is mortal, our soul remains pure and untouched.

CHAPTER EIGHTEEN

❦

Ishwara (God) and the Jiva (Individual soul)

The Bhagavad Gita 17th chapter is a beautiful summation of Upanishadic thought and the classical yoga system of spiritual practice. It is often explained that Upanishads are the philosophical basis of the Gita, and the chapter focuses largely on a synthesis of the two schools of thought. In this chapter, the Lord reveals to Arjuna the famous Virat-Rupa Darshana, a spectacular vision of His divine cosmic form.

The Bhagavad Gita chapter 17 starts with the praises of the Lord, naming Him as the destroyer of fear and ultimate refuge. This idea resonates with many verses in the Upanishads, where it is said that the Lord is the ultimate source of fearlessness and refuge.

The chapter further explains the relationship between Ishwara (God) and the jiva (individual soul). It explains that Ishwara is the source and authority of the jiva, and that the jiva's nature is essentially an intimate relationship with Shiva. If one knows and loves Him as the innermost Self, that person will be liberated. This idea is also found in the Upanishads, such as in the Chandogya Upanishad

8.7.1 which states that "one who knows the Self attains immortality".

The chapter also speaks of the Lord as the source of brahman (Absolute Reality). The Lord identifies Himself as the source and ultimate cause of all things, manifesting as the supramental being, beyond all individual souls and material things. This teaching is a recurring theme in the Upanishads. For example, the Taittiriya Upanishad 3.1 states, "Brahman is life, and eternal, it is beyond evil and death".

The chapter also speaks of yoga and the yoga methods used to reach the Supreme destination. This is an idea which is found in many of the primary Upanishads, such as in the Brihadaranyaka Upanishad 6.3.3 where it is stated, "Yoga is the means of union with Iswara".

The Bhagavad Gita chapter 17 is truly a beautiful articulation of Upanishadic thought, explaining ideas such the nature of Ishwara, the relationship between Ishwara and the jiva, the source of brahman, and the importance of yoga. Taken together, this chapter provides an important insight into the Upanishadic tradition and the Way of Liberation.

CHAPTER NINETEEN

❦

The Path of Knowledge

The Bhagavat Gita is a revered Hindu scripture which is considered to be part of the Upanishads, a collection of ancient spiritual texts. The eighteenth chapter of the Bhagavat Gita is especially significant, as it highlights its connection with the Upanishads.

The Bhagavat Gita's eighteenth chapter is entitled "The Path of Knowledge" and is mainly composed of a discourse between Lord Krishna, considered to be the embodiment of Supreme Consciousness, and Arjuna, a great warrior and one of Lord Krishna's closest disciples. Here, Lord Krishna encourages Arjuna to discard all fear, doubts, and negative thoughts noting that "all works are accomplished based on how you think". He then lays out paths of knowledge leading to the attainment of the ultimate spiritual enlightenment.

This chapter makes the connection to the Upanishads explicit: Krishna presents the beloved Upanishadic discourse on knowledge, the path of contemplation and inquiry, and the practice of yoga. He outlines the timeless practices of knowledge or "Jnana Yoga" and encourages Arjuna to give up all attachment and live in samadhi (oneness) with the divine will, a practice described as "Karma Yoga". The Bhagavat Gita's eighteenth chapter is thus a profound Upanishadic reflection, reiterating the Vedantic truth that the human being's purpose is to know thyself and to reunite with the divine.

Moreover, Lord Krishna opens with a reference to the sacred Om and speaks of sravana, manana and nididhyasana, the three means of attaining knowledge described in the Upanishads. Through sravana, the seeker hears of the divinity, through manana he reflects on it within himself, and through nididhyasana, the seeker realizes his oneness with the divine. In reminders such as this, the Bhagavat Gita's eighteenth chapter reinforces the Upanishadic teachings and expresses its alignment with them.

The importance of the Upanishads lies in their reminder that the divine exists within each individual and is expressed through knowledge and self-realization. Chapter eighteen of the Bhagavat Gita does an excellent job of reiterating this timeless truth and upholding the wisdom found in the ancient Upanishadic texts. The Bhagavat Gita's eighteenth chapter teaches us to dive deep, to authentically question and not unthinkingly follow tradition and dogma, and to truly understand one's ultimate purpose and relationship with the divine.

CHAPTER TWENTY

SUMMARY

The Bhagavad Gita and the Upanishad are two of India's most important ancient texts and share a deep spiritual connection. Found in the Mahabharata, the Bhagavad Gita is an ancient dialogue between Krishna, the supreme being, and Arjuna, a warrior on the battlefield. Through this dialogue, Krishna reveals the ultimate path of salvation and how to find true peace and wisdom. Similarly, the Upanishads, a series of over 200 Sanskrit texts, contain spiritual teachings which share similar themes with the Bhagavad Gita.

The Bhagavad Gita is a message of spiritual truth and has been a source of inspiration, motivation and guidance to many over the ages. Its teachings are simple: live a life of devotion, compassion and inner peace. The Bhagavad Gita is centered around the concept of Dharma, the moral law of nature and one's personal moral duty. It states one must follow the path of Dharma and do what is right and good for themselves and for others.

The Upanishads center around the concept of Brahman, or the Supreme Reality. It is within this concept that all things exist and from which all things originate. The Upanishads also teach that one must strive for moksha, the liberation from samsara, the endless cycle of rebirth. The path to liberation is the Atman, or soul, which is within all living things. Through spiritual enlightenment, the Atman can be united with Brahman, or the Supreme Reality.

The Bhagavad Gita and Upanishads share certain common teachings, such as the importance of living in harmony with nature, developing compassion and love for all living things, and the need for spiritual enlightenment. Both emphasize the importance of inner peace and simplicity, and understanding one's true nature and inner self.

The two texts are also linked in their view of Dharma, the moral law of nature, and moksha, the liberation from samsara. The Bhagavad Gita teaches that one must strive to do what is right and good in order to find peace in life, while the Upanishads teach that one must strive for moksha, or liberation from samsara, in order to find true freedom. Ultimately, both texts point towards the potential for spiritual enlightenment, which ultimately leads to inner peace and true freedom.

In conclusion, the Bhagavad Gita and Upanishads share a deep spiritual connection and relationship. Through their teachings, the two ancient texts offer a path for spiritual enlightenment and true peace. Most importantly, these texts serve as a reminder that true inner peace and freedom can be attained through devotion and an understanding of one's true nature.

Other Books Of The Author

1. The Moments When I Met God (English)
2. Kashiyile Theertha Pathangal (Malayalam)
3. GURU GYAN VANI (Hindi)
4. Abhiprerak Gita (Hindi)
5. ASSI SE JAIN GHAT TAK (Hindi)
6. Hopelessness of Arjuna (English)
7. The Soul and It's True Nature (English)
8. Sense of Action (Karma)(English)
9. Action through Wisdom (English)
10. Action through Wisdom (English)
11. THEORY AND PRACTICAL OF EVERY ACTION (English)
12. LOGICAL UNDERSTANDING OF THE SUPREME (English)
13. THE IMPERISHABLE SUPREME (English)
14. Yatra Nishadraj se Hanuman Ghat Tak (Hindi)
15. Yatra Karnatak Ghat se Raja Ghat Tak (Hindi)
16. Yatra Pandey Ghat se Prayagraj Ghat Tak (Hindi)
17. Yatra Ranjendra Prasad Ghat se Dattatreya Ghat Tak (Hindi)
18. YaatraSindhiya Ghat se Gwaliar Ghat Tak (Hindi)
19. Yatra Mangala Gauri Ghat se Hanuman Gadhi Ghat Tak (Hindi)
20. Yatra Gaay Ghat Se Nishad Ghat Tak (Hindi)
21. MAA GANGA, GHATEN EVM UTSAV (Hindi)
22. Ganga Arti Dev Deepavali evam Any Utsav (Hindi)
23. Potentials of Digitalized India (English)
24. VEDIC CONSCIOUSNESS (English)
25. A Brief Introduction to Vedic Science (English)

OTHER BOOKS OF THE AUTHOR

26. Kashi ke Barah Jyotirling (Hindi)
27. IMPACT OF MOTIVATION (English)
28. Let's have a Milky Way Journey
29. Color Therapy in a Nutshell
30. Rigveda in a Nutshell
31. Yajurveda in a Nutshell
32. Samveda in a Nutshell
33. Atharva Veda in a Nutshell
34. Ayurveda in a Nutshell
35. Srimad Bhagavad Gita and Upanishad Connection

Contact

DR. JAGADEESH PILLAI

PhD in Vedic Science

Four Times Guinness World Record Holder

Winner of Mahatma Gandhi Vishwa Shanti Puraskar and Global Peace Ambassador

9839093003

myrichindia@gmail.com

drjagadeeshpillai@facebook

drjagadeeshpillai@instagram

jagadeeshpillai@youtube

www.JAGADEESHPILLAI.com